ALL THE COLORS OF ME

PICTURING MY SADNESS

KNOWING AND SHOWING MY FEELINGS THROUGH ART

ANNA SHEPHERD
illustrated by ALICIA MÁS

PowerKiDS press.

Published in 2027
by The Rosen Publishing Group, Inc.
2544 Clinton Street, Buffalo, NY 14224

First published in Great Britain in 2023 by Hodder & Stoughton

Credits

Series Editor: Grace Glendinning
Series Designer: Alicia Más
Illustrations: Alicia Más

Cataloging-in-Publication Data

Names: Shepherd, Anna, author. | Más, Alicia, illustrator.
Title: Picturing my sadness / Anna Shepherd, illustrated by Alicia Más.
Description: Buffalo, New York : PowerKids Press, 2027. | Series: All the colors of me
Identifiers: ISBN 9781499458855 (pbk.) | ISBN 9781499458862 (library bound) | ISBN 9781499458879 (ebook)
Subjects: LCSH: Sadness in children--Juvenile literature. | Sadness--Juvenile literature. | Emotions--Juvenile literature.
Classification: LCC BF723.S15 S547 2027 | DDC 155.4124--dc23

Printed in China

CPSIA Compliance Information: Batch #QS27PK. For further information contact Rosen Publishing at 1-800-237-9932.

CONTENTS

LISTENING TO SADNESS

It is really important to listen to our feelings. Sadness is part of being human – we all feel it. It comes by now and then to help.

It visits to show us that we **need a hug** from someone we love or maybe that we need to **ask for help** with a problem.

Our sadness can help us feel more grateful for the happy things in life.

And when we've felt sad ourselves, it helps us be more caring when we see others feeling down.

But **it's tricky** if we don't know **why** sadness has appeared, or if we can't **move on** from it.

SOMETIMES WE NEED A LITTLE HELP!

Can you think of some things you've done in the past to help yourself feel better when you were sad?

ART-MAKING CAN HELP

Doing art is a great way to understand and deal with sadness. The pages of this book will help you to see how.

Art gives us a creative way to explain our sadness because ...

... when we are sad, finding the right words can be **hard** ...

... and sometimes we have lots of words, but saying them aloud feels **impossible.**

Art also lets us **create a different world** where we **feel safe** to **share our sad thoughts** (with a little help from our imagination).

And sometimes just doodling, painting, or building something can help the sadness lift away altogether.

LOTS OF FAMOUS ARTISTS HAVE MADE ART TO HELP THEM COPE WITH SADNESS.

You might think, "But I'm no good at art!" (Impossible!) But you don't have to worry about what it will look like. It is all about DOING. Then we see how the DOING helps us understand our feelings.

So let's get creative and see what happens!

We can start by using art to get to know sadness a bit better.

SADNESS IS ...

a natural response to lots of different things, and is different for everyone.

What upsets you might not make someone else feel that way.

Begin by getting to know your particular sorts of sadness: sketch a few pictures of things that have made you sad in the past.

Colors and textures that feel sad to you might feel scary or exciting to someone else!

And sometimes our sadness feels **sharp and fast**; sometimes it's **heavy or dull**.

Can you add colors, textures, and shades to each of your sketches? Try to show each sadness in its own unique way.

Starting to DESCRIBE your different sadnesses HELPS you SEE them more CLEARLY.

We can also use our pictures to think about what our

SADNESS FEELS LIKE.

Close your eyes and imagine jumping into one of your sadness memory sketches.

Can you remember **how your body felt** when the sadness happened?

Did your eyes feel WATERY? Did it feel HEAVY over your HEART?

Make a **"sadness hot spot"** picture.

If you can, head outside with a friend. Trace around each other in chalk and mark **all the bits of you that feel sadness.** Do you feel it in your toes, nose, tummy, elbow?

Here is mine:

Take a photo of your drawing so you can remember to **listen to these parts of your body.** They are giving you **clues** about your sadness.

If you spot the sad feelings starting in your body, lie down and imagine a warm rain washing away the chalk hot spots.

Focus on your **breathing** and, if you like, put your **hand on your heart or tummy**.

You can also say to yourself **something** like,

"This SADNESS will PASS."

Afterwards, it can be a good idea to make some more art about this moment when you have looked after your sadness.

Art can act like a magic mirror to help us see what our

SADNESS LOOKS LIKE.

Sadness on your face might look like this:

Have you ever looked in the mirror when you are upset? Grab paper and something to draw with. Create a self-portrait of your "sad face." What colors would you use? What are your eyes doing? Your forehead? Your nose, chin, cheeks?

Picturing sadness ITSELF can also help us to understand this gloomy visitor a bit better.

Do you see sadness as a simple shape or a pattern? Is it something from nature – waves, snow, or a tree?

Or is sadness a creature? What might it look like? Does the creature have anything it wants to say?

Getting familiar with your sad face and your sadness visitor can help you to spot the feeling more quickly.

Just as we all feel sadness differently, we all **show** it differently too! So, do you know what your

SADNESS ACTS LIKE?

When we are sad, we might want to ...

... CRY or SOB or WAIL AMONG FRIENDS ...

... or have a QUIET CUDDLE with SOMEONE WE TRUST.

Or maybe HIDING under the blanket alone is just the right thing!

Sometimes our sadness comes out in an **angry** voice or action. It's a bit **confusing!** It can be **really hard** for other people to see the sadness **hiding** underneath the **explosion**.

To help yourself and others figure out what you need when you're sad, you can make a set of puppets to suit each sadness:

TODAY I AM A TORTOISE WHO NEEDS A MOMENT IN MY SHELL TO CALM DOWN.

THIS CUDDLY CATERPILLAR NEEDS A HUG!

THE LION CAME OUT TODAY.
I NEED A BIG ROAR AND A CHAT TO UNDERSTAND WHAT'S WRONG.

Now let's get even better at spotting the different

SHADES OF SADNESS

that come to call.

Here are some great words to describe different sizes of sadness:

LONELY
MISERABLE
DISAPPOINTED
DEPRESSED
GLOOMY
HOPELESS

Start creating your own personal **Sadness Scale** so you can keep an eye on **how powerful your sadness is** as you face it, and as you work through it.

GIVE A NAME TO EACH LEVEL OF SADNESS. DECORATE THE WORDS IN DIFFERENT STYLES. THEN DRAW A DIFFERENT UNHAPPY FACE TO GO WITH EACH WORD.

When you next feel sad, look at the faces. **Which one most looks like how you feel?**

How about after you have cried or talked to someone, done some art or breathing exercises? Has it changed?

Your Sadness Scale shows you that we can change the power of our sadness and even move on from sadness altogether, with some practice (or some help, see pages 20–21).

It may take some time, so be patient with yourself.

SUPER-SAD

MISERABLE

6 7 8 9 10

Sometimes our sadness is so big that

SPEAKING OF SADNESS

at all feels too overwhelming.

When you can't form the words to explain your sadness, it can really help to start making some art and see where it takes you.

You may end up being quite **surprised** by what you have drawn!

At times, writing out or drawing what's going on in our heads can be clearer than what our mouths or bodies are saying.

Don't want to write it out? You could **act** it out instead – drama is art too! Create a scene with a trusted friend or adult, or you can even let your favorite toy do all the talking in a puppet show.

So, what do you do when you've tried lots of ideas, but you just

CAN'T STOP THE SADNESS?

Sometimes sadness can feel like it's everywhere – too much to hold inside or send away.

Sadness is not ours alone to deal with, because when it's all tucked up inside, it might feel a bit like this:

But **once we have got it out and looked at it with someone who can help**, we might realize it's actually a bit more like this:

We can help ourselves spot when sadness is getting too big for us.

Keep an **art journal** so you can **look back** and see how **your art changes** when you are feeling **different emotions**.

On the harder days, ask yourself:

How did you react to the big sadness? Did you cry, stomp, or shout? Did you want to be alone or with someone? How did people around you respond?

IMPORTANT! If you feel a sadness that doesn't go away, speak to a trusted adult who can introduce you to someone who is trained to help people with hard feelings. You might feel a bit embarrassed or confused, but be kind to yourself. This is an important emotion and we ALL feel like this sometimes.

PRACTICING SADNESS

means getting in the habit of knowing and showing how we feel.

Just like with anything, practice really helps.

Art can be really handy at helping you to remember to keep your new habit going. Let's make some **decorative reminders** to put up somewhere safe. You could try tacking up a **checklist:**

MY SADNESS CHECKLIST

1. Do I know WHY this sadness is here?
2. What usually works to make me FEEL BETTER?
   - MAKING A COLLAGE
   - PAINTING WITH MY HANDS
   - MESSY BAKING
3. What do my brain and heart need to HEAR or SEE right now?

Or what about some **"truth note" reminders?** We really do **listen to the words in our heads**, so why not make them **kind words?**

Write them down, decorate them, and tack them up somewhere you will see them often.

WHAT do you think you would really like to HEAR WHEN you are FEELING SAD?

I CAN MOVE ON FROM SADNESS!

Or if words aren't your thing, how about putting up a poster filled with drawings or photos of the things that make you smile or feel warm on the inside?

YOU ARE A SADNESS ARTIST!

There are so many ways to be creative when you feel sad, and now that you've read this book, you are an expert feelings artist!

Here are even more fun ideas to keep your creativity flowing, and your sadness in balance.

Decorating a mask can be a great way to **ask for help** with a **hidden sadness.**

It can also be a relief to make a **big, messy picture without worrying** what it will look like! *Get an adult's permission first and put on some old clothes. Doing it outside might be a good idea!*

What about using your **fingers in the paint?**

Does the feeling of paint between your fingers help you feel calm?

Someone very wise said that knowing what to do with your feelings is a **SUPERPOWER.**

Strengthening that power will help you all your life!

Can you design a superhero who knows just how to deal with your sadness? What costume would they wear? What are their superpowers?

Some people enjoy making art that looks realistic. Do you? Can you make a picture about your sad feelings that is really detailed?

Other people like making images that use just colors, shapes, and lines. It's not about looking like something real, but can show very real feelings. Why not give it a try?

Mandalas are an example of this kind of art. They are usually **circular pieces** of art that have **repeating shapes** and can be any color or pattern that suits your mood.

MANDALAS are used all over the world for HELPING people UNDERSTAND THEMSELVES and THE WORLD around them a bit better.

Can you think of other ways to make fun art? I think you have a BIG imagination, ready for MANY different shades of sadness.

KEY TERMS

Balance: when emotions are steady, even, and stable.

Collage: a type of art using different materials pieced together to create an image.

Creativity: using your imagination to make something.

Depressed: feeling very low and as if you can't escape the sadness. It can affect your eating, sleeping and energy levels.

Mandala: a circle-shaped piece of detailed art that helps the artist practice mindfulness and consider the universe.

Overwhelming: when a feeling is very strong and it becomes hard to cope.

Pattern: a design or detail that is repeated.

Portrait: an image of a person.

Shades: slightly different varieties of something, such as a color.

Sketch: a simple or quick version of a creative idea.

Texture: the feel or look of the surface of something.

BOOKS TO READ

***Kids Can Cope* series,**
by Gill Hasson (Franklin Watts)

- *Bounce Back from Disappointment*
- *Face Your Fears*
- *Let Go of Jealousy*
- *Put Your Worries Away*
- *Say Hi When You're Shy*
- *Step Back from Frustration*
- *Take Charge of Anger*
- *Turn Away from Teasing*

***A World Full of Feelings* series,**
by Louise Spilsbury (Franklin Watts)

- *Finding Calm*
- *Finding Courage*
- *Finding Happiness*
- *Finding Kindness*

***Build Resilience* series,**
by Honor Head (Franklin Watts)

- *Anxiety and Self-esteem*
- *Coping with Change*
- *Friendships and Bullying*
- *Unexpected Challenges*

WEBSITES to **VISIT** with the help of an adult:

Headspace.com

A website and app offering meditation and mindfulness tools to expand on the practice of understanding and dealing with emotions.

Youthmindfulness.org

Resources for mindfulness programs for young people.

HOW TO USE THIS BOOK: A GUIDE FOR ADULTS

This series of art therapy books has been developed to provide a creative starting point for further discussion and exploration around children's emotions.

Each book is intended for children to **share** with trusted adults, whether one-on-one or in a group setting in the classroom or elsewhere.

This book, *Picturing My Sadness*, is a careful exploration of the look and feel of all kinds of sadness. When dealing with any tricky emotion, big or small, the utmost priority is making children feel **safe and heard** as they think things through.

Whether sharing at home or in a group setting, plan to begin at a time when you and your child or group are relaxed and have an uninterrupted moment to share an activity. It is important that the adult leading the activity is emotionally available when sitting to do this. This can be hard when you feel rushed and stressed, so choose the timing carefully.

Only you will know how much time and energy you and your child or group are able to give to this practice in each session, and what will suit your setting – dip in; read it completely; return to it again at times in the future. No matter what, **don't push things** – try out the bits that your child or group are most drawn to. Have a go at different activities when they feel right for the progression of the individual or group. Use each approach at a time and place that is **most helpful**.

The activities are catalysts for conversations about how children feel. Once the creativity starts flowing, the session may well grow beyond what's in these pages. Maybe a child has their own ideas about ways to feel a bit better that they could share with you or the group? Try to **listen** and not offer unwelcome solutions or critiques. It can be hard when you want to help, but trust that **with love, support, and encouragement,** children can usually find their own way through.

Also, take **notice of your own feelings** and responses as your child or group creates, and be mindful that you are modelling how to manage and regulate emotions. You do not need to get it right all the time; **be kind to yourself**, just as we encourage the children to be throughout this book. Helping children is not always easy.

In a group setting it is very important to make sure every child feels safe to share and participate. Establish a rapport of **support** and **zero judgement** of their art and expression of emotion.

But keep in mind that some children may need to have additional, dedicated help beyond what is appropriate to do on your own in a classroom or group setting. See page 32 for quick-reference contacts if you feel your child or group member needs further professional or anonymous assistance.

If you are concerned that a child is struggling to cope, then it is worth seeking advice from a professional.

American Art Therapy Association
arttherapy.org/art-therapist-locator

Learn more about art therapy and find a trained therapist to continue emotional work with a creative approach.

Find a Warmline
www.warmline.org

Warmlines are confidential, free phone services that offer emotional support to people who just need someone to talk to. Find a Warmline near you here.

Kids Help Phone
1-800-668-6868
kidshelpphone.ca

Kids Help Phone is a Canadian e-mental health service for youths with counselors available 24 hours a day.

National Mental Health Hotline
1-866-903-3787
mentalhealthhotline.org

This free, 24-hour help line connects people in need with caring, knowledgeable, licensed mental health counselors.

Nemours Kids Health
kidshealth.org

This website is full of helpful health resources for parents, kids, teens, and educators.